Hawaiian Magic

Rod Morris

Learning Media

Contents

Introduction

There's something very special about an island. These specks of land surrounded by water – sometimes whole oceans of it – can seem mysterious and exciting places. Each island is a little world of its own, separate and quite different from any other place. The plants and animals that live on these islands are often very different from others of their kind, too.

For me, the most magical of all islands
are the islands of Hawaii.

Kauai

Niihau
Kaula

Oahu

Molokai

Lanai

Maui

Pacific
Ocean

Kahoolawe

Hawaii

United States
of America

Los Angeles

Hawaiian islands

1. The Birth of an Island

Many islands that are famous for their beaches, like those around Hawaii, began life as volcanoes on the seafloor. Far beneath the waves, **molten** rock erupted from inside Earth, and a mountain began to grow. It kept on growing with new eruptions until finally the top of the mountain appeared above the ocean, and a new island was born.

On the lower slopes of a new volcanic island, if the water is warm and clear, **coral** will start to grow just below the ocean's surface. Gradually, it will form a white ring around the island. This becomes a coral **reef**.

If you visit the Big Island of Hawaii, you can still find active volcanoes and see molten rock bubbling out of holes in the ground. You can even have a special barbecue over the red-hot rocks! But you'll need a long stick – the heat coming off the rocks is so intense that you can quickly get burned if you stand too close.

The highest volcano on the Big Island of Hawaii is Mauna Kea. If you measured the height of Mauna Kea from its peak down to its base on the bottom of the sea, it would be taller than Mount Everest. Even in the tropical summer, its peak can be covered in snow.

Mauna Kea is 31,796 feet (5.6 miles) high from the ocean floor to its summit (it's 13,796 feet above sea level). Mount Everest is 29,028 feet (5.5 miles) high above sea level.

Mauna Kea		Mount Everest
	31,796 ft	
	29,028 ft	
	18,000 ft	
ocean floor	0 ft — sea level	

2. New Arrivals

Getting to an island across all that water can be difficult if you're an animal or a plant. Some of the first arrivals on a new volcanic island are often creatures who live at sea. The animals that first reached the islands of Hawaii thousands of years ago were either very good fliers, like the seabirds, or very good swimmers, like the turtles and the seals. You can still spot some of these creatures on quieter beaches around Hawaii today.

The Magic of an Island

When a new island first rises out of the ocean, it's just a pile of hot rock. After a while, it cools, and then visitors start arriving. Plant seeds wash up onto the shore or are carried in the wind. Seabirds land for a rest, and turtles and seals check it out. Flying insects blow in on the wind, too.

But the new island is usually very different from the lands that these visitors came from, and, if they stay, many of them die. But some of them – the ones that are a little bit better suited to their new home – manage to survive. Centuries go by, and the island animals and plants end up looking very different from the way their ancestors looked. I like to think of this as "island magic."

The Philip Island Hibiscus grows only on one tiny island off the coast of Norfolk Island.

The tiny blue lorikeet lives in the coconut palms on a coral island near Tahiti.

A weevil from the island of New Guinea.

The hibiscus, lorikeet, and weevil are examples of island magic at work. They made it to their islands over huge expanses of water by being good fliers or having seeds that could travel long distances easily.

Just as these plants and animals have changed with island life, those in the Hawaiian islands have changed, too. In the next few chapters, we'll meet some of the plants and animals that are **unique** to the Hawaiian islands.

3. Lucky Arrivals

Traveling Trees

Some visitors to the Hawaiian islands may have just been lucky to end up there – like the coconut palm. When a ripe coconut falls from its tree onto a beach somewhere, the tide can carry it out to sea. The **husk** of the coconut helps it to float, and ocean currents can carry it thousands of miles.

If it's lucky enough to be washed ashore somewhere, the young coconut may take root in the ground. Perhaps a new tree will grow, thousands of miles from its parent tree, on a new island.

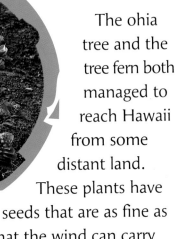

Ohia tree

The ohia tree and the tree fern both managed to reach Hawaii from some distant land. These plants have seeds that are as fine as dust and so light that the wind can carry them for miles. Most of these wind-borne seeds would have landed in the sea and died, but a few lucky ones reached the bare rocks of the island volcano and were tough enough to grow. They had the whole place to themselves. They grew into great forests where other traveling plants and animals could find food and shelter from the sun.

Tree fern

Tarweed Transformation

North American tarweed

Another plant whose seeds were lucky enough to reach the Hawaiian islands thousands of years ago, was the North American tarweed. There weren't many other kinds of plants on the islands then, so there was lots of room for its seeds to spread.

In each place that the tarweed seeds landed, the soil and the living conditions were a little different. Over time, the tarweeds that grew in different places became different from other tarweeds. On one island, a tarweed managed to become a tree, and on another, it slowly changed into a creeping vine.

Tarweed tree

The silversword that grows on the Hawaiian island of Maui today is very different from its ancestor the tarweed. This famous Hawaiian plant looks almost like it's from another planet. Its spiky leaves are covered in silvery hairs to protect it from the hot sun. Just under the surface of the sand, its fine roots collect the dew that falls on the ground each night. The plant stores this precious water in its fleshy leaves, just like a cactus.

After many years, when the silversword has stored up enough food and water, it sends up an enormous flowery spike, about 5 feet tall. The flowers are colored bright pink so that they attract insects. When an insect finds a silversword in flower, it feeds on the nectar and **pollinates** many flowers. The silversword's hundreds of flowers produce millions of seeds. In this hot, dry area, only one or two will be lucky enough to find cool crevices and grow into new silverswords.

Another island tarweed that lives on Maui Island is the greensword. It looks a lot like the silversword, but it lives in an area where there is way too much water. So the greensword doesn't need hairs on its leaves, and it doesn't need fleshy leaves. There are plenty of insects where it grows, so the flowers don't need to advertise themselves with bright colors. Instead, they are small, and they hang their heads down so that they don't get wet.

4. Hawaiian Living

When you enter the cool forests on the Hawaiian islands today, you might think that they're much like other forests. But they're not because there are no **native** earthworms or ants living here. These creatures couldn't swim or fly across the ocean. So insect travelers that arrived here long ago, like damselflies and moths, found a land without their old enemies, the ants. They began living very different lives, and little by little, they began to change.

The **larvae** of Hawaiian damselflies climbed out of the ponds and streams where they had always lived and moved up to live in the treetops. With no ants to hunt them, and no ants to hunt their insect neighbors, they became hunters themselves.

Damselfly larvae

A damselfly

Carnivorous Caterpillars

Some of the caterpillars changed, too. Caterpillars eat leaves everywhere in the world, but in the Hawaiian islands, about nine kinds of caterpillars stopped eating leaves. Instead, they began catching and eating the insects that would normally have been eaten by the ants.

It's not unusual for an insect to experiment like this when it arrives on an island and finds a different environment from what it's used to. So island living can turn a plant-eating caterpillar into a fierce hunter.

5. Hawaiian Cousins

Adaptable Ducks

Thousands of years ago, traveling ducks reached Laysan Island, which is one of the Hawaiian islands that lies in the north of the group. Although ducks usually feed in the water, there was very little food in the saltwater ponds where they landed. The ducks that survived were those that learned to feed in the air, like land birds. So now, Laysan ducks eat flies.

Laysan ducks are smaller than their ancestors, perhaps so that they don't need to eat as much food since food can be limited on an island. Islands often create dwarfs like this – and giants too. Ferns growing in the forests on Hawaii have become as large as trees because they haven't had much competition from other trees.

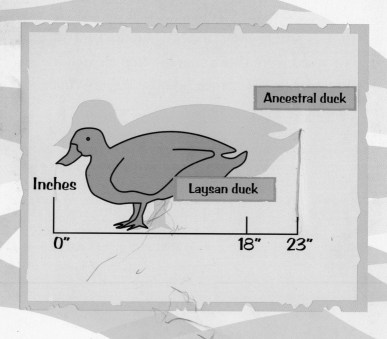

Ancestral duck

Inches

Laysan duck

0"   18"   23"

Island animals and plants can change their appearance in other ways too. The Hawaiian goose still looks similar to the goose that first came from North America thousands of years ago. But now that they live around Hawaii's dry volcanic mountains instead of on ponds and rivers, these island geese walk a lot more and swim very little. Therefore, they don't need **webbing** between their toes anymore, and it's gradually starting to disappear.

Fancy Finches

The way that flowers, plants, insects, and animals have changed to suit island living has happened with small birds too.

Many of the little birds in the forests of Hawaii today are close cousins of the first finch. But these island finches look quite different from each other. Some have green or black or red feathers, and their beaks can be thick or thin, long or short, or even curved or straight.

They all eat different things too. The first finches arrived in the Hawaiian islands years before other kinds of small birds, so they were free to try out all kinds of food that they wouldn't normally eat. This meant that, over time, the shape of their beaks changed to suit the kind of food they ate.

The finches that eat insects have short, thin, straight beaks. Those that eat seeds have short, fat, straight beaks. One of the finches has a beak like a parrot and is called the parrotbill. Other finches called honeycreepers have long, curved beaks that they use to sip nectar from flowers.

The Hawaiian islands are home to some of the world's strangest animals and plants. Thousands of years of island living has transformed them into creatures that are very different from their ancestors who arrived there long ago. This is what makes the islands of Hawaii so magical.